EMERSON HANCOCK

ChatGPT for Journalists

Enhance Reporting and Streamline
News Production with AI-Powered Tools
(2024 Guide)

Copyright © 2024 by Emerson Hancock

All rights reserved. No part of this publication may be reproduced, stored or transmitted in any form or by any means, electronic, mechanical, photocopying, recording, scanning, or otherwise without written permission from the publisher. It is illegal to copy this book, post it to a website, or distribute it by any other means without permission.

First edition

*This book was professionally typeset on Reedsy.
Find out more at reedsy.com*

Contents

1. Introducing ChatGPT for Journalists — 1
2. Utilizing ChatGPT for Research and Investigation — 3
3. Utilizing ChatGPT for Writing and Editing News Pieces — 6
4. Fact-checking with ChatGPT — 9
5. Using ChatGPT for Interviews and Reporting — 11
6. Utilizing ChatGPT for Data Journalism and Visualization — 14
7. Social Media and Citizen Journalism — 17
8. Crisis Reporting and Risk Management — 20
9. Ethical Concerns in AI-Aided Journalism — 23
10. Looking Ahead: ChatGPT and the Future of Journalism — 27

1

Introducing ChatGPT for Journalists

ChatGPT, developed by OpenAI, serves as a valuable tool for journalists, offering support in multiple aspects such as generating article ideas, aiding in research, fact-checking, and more. This segment delves into how journalists can integrate ChatGPT into their workflow to elevate their reporting.

Journalism demands creativity, critical analysis, and impeccable writing prowess. However, the digital era has reshaped journalism dynamics, leading to a surge in content production, tighter deadlines, and a focus on clicks and shares. Consequently, journalists seek ways to boost productivity and efficiency without compromising quality. This is where AI solutions like ChatGPT step in, assisting journalists in streamlining their processes, refining research and writing skills, and ultimately crafting compelling narratives.

In the subsequent sections, we will explore the diverse applications of ChatGPT in empowering journalists to excel in their field.

Understanding ChatGPT

ChatGPT, developed by OpenAI, is a sophisticated language model proficient in producing responses that closely resemble human-written text. It operates on the GPT (Generative Pretrained Transformer) framework, enabling it to comprehend and generate natural language across various contexts. By training on extensive internet data, ChatGPT acquires the ability to recognize and mimic linguistic patterns and styles. Consequently, it finds utility in journalism, where it can aid in research, inspire story concepts, and streamline certain writing processes.

The Role of AI in Journalism

The involvement of AI in journalism is swiftly advancing and adapting. AI's capabilities extend to automating tasks once performed manually, such as fact-checking, interview transcription, and data analysis. Furthermore, it can contribute to generating news articles, condensing lengthy texts, and discerning patterns and trends within vast datasets. AI presents journalists with opportunities to save time, improve accuracy, and effectively cover significant stories. However, concerns persist regarding AI's influence on journalism's future, including issues of potential bias and the displacement of jobs due to increased automation.

2

Utilizing ChatGPT for Research and Investigation

ChatGPT serves as a valuable asset for journalists in their research and investigative endeavors. AI models like ChatGPT possess the capability to process and sift through extensive data sets, aiding journalists in swiftly pinpointing crucial information and emerging trends.

Moreover, ChatGPT facilitates journalists in pinpointing potential interviewees or subject matter experts by analyzing online content to discern individuals with relevant expertise and provide their contact details. Furthermore, it assists journalists in fact-checking their work by scrutinizing sources and cross-referencing information, thereby identifying any inconsistencies or inaccuracies, which is instrumental in upholding the accuracy and reliability of journalistic content.

Nonetheless, it's imperative to acknowledge that while AI tools such as ChatGPT are beneficial, they should be regarded as supplementary rather than substitutive to conventional journalistic skills. Journalists must continue to conduct their own research, validate sources, and meticulously fact-check their work to uphold the highest standards of accuracy and integrity.

Enhancing the Research Process with AI

ChatGPT emerges as a valuable ally for journalists in streamlining the research process. With its adeptness at swiftly and efficiently navigating through extensive data sets, it aids journalists in uncovering patterns and connections that might have otherwise eluded detection. For instance, journalists can leverage ChatGPT to swiftly sift through copious government documents or public records to unearth pertinent information for their narratives.

Additionally, ChatGPT aids journalists in source identification and verification. Its capacity to analyze text and language assists in detecting linguistic patterns indicative of a source's authenticity or trustworthiness. Furthermore, it helps in identifying potential conflicts of interest or other factors that could impact a source's credibility.

In summary, ChatGPT empowers journalists to conduct more comprehensive and efficient research, ultimately leading to more precise and informative reporting.

Delving Deeper into Data Analysis

In today's landscape of abundant data, journalists are presented with a treasure trove of information that holds the potential to unveil narratives and trends that might have eluded detection otherwise. However, this data often poses a challenge due to its complexity, requiring specialized tools for analysis. This is precisely where AI and ChatGPT come into play.

By harnessing the power of AI for data analysis, journalists can efficiently navigate through vast datasets to pinpoint patterns, correlations, and anomalies. This capability enables them to unearth fresh perspectives on stories, pinpoint potential sources, and establish connections among disparate pieces of information. For instance, AI-driven analysis could be utilized to scrutinize financial records for suspicious transactions or to dissect social media activity to detect emerging trends or issues.

Moreover, ChatGPT can serve as a valuable asset for journalists in tackling fundamental research tasks. It can swiftly generate background information on specific topics, locate pertinent sources, or highlight key themes and subjects relevant to a story. This streamlined assistance not only saves journalists time but also empowers them to concentrate on the crux of their work.

In essence, the synergy between AI and ChatGPT holds immense promise in bolstering the research and investigative prowess of journalists, facilitating the discovery of new stories and insights with greater speed and efficiency.

3

Utilizing ChatGPT for Writing and Editing News Pieces

ChatGPT offers valuable support for journalists engaged in crafting and refining news articles. Below are several ways in which ChatGPT can contribute to this process:

1. Summarizing articles: ChatGPT can analyze news pieces and deliver concise summaries of their key points. This functionality proves beneficial for journalists requiring swift assessments for research or fact-validation purposes.
2. Crafting headlines: ChatGPT can propose headlines based on the content of news stories, thus saving journalists time in devising engaging headlines that accurately capture the essence of the story.
3. Fact-validation: ChatGPT can verify the accuracy of news articles. By entering a claim or statement, ChatGPT swiftly assesses data to either corroborate or challenge the assertion.
4. Writing support: ChatGPT offers recommendations for sentence structure, grammar, and vocabulary in news writing. Such assistance proves invaluable for journalists facing tight deadlines or seeking aid in their writing.

5. Plagiarism detection: ChatGPT can identify instances of plagiarism in news content by comparing a journalist's writing against a vast database of articles.
6. Editing and proofreading: ChatGPT aids in editing and proofreading news stories by suggesting revisions to enhance clarity, conciseness, and overall quality.

Creating Articles with AI Assistance

ChatGPT serves as a valuable resource for journalists when drafting news articles with AI assistance. Journalists can leverage the AI model to generate initial concepts, refine story angles, and suggest relevant interview sources. Additionally, it aids in outlining and structuring articles, identifying potential biases, and enhancing the accuracy of news stories.

However, it's crucial to recognize that AI should not replace the journalistic skills of research, source verification, and fact-checking. Journalists must verify any information produced by AI before publishing it as news. The AI model should function as a supportive tool, complementing journalists' expertise and critical thinking rather than supplanting them.

Utilizing ChatGPT for Editing and Proofreading

In the journalistic process, editing and proofreading play pivotal roles, and ChatGPT emerges as a beneficial aid in both domains. Below are various ways through which ChatGPT can contribute to editing and proofreading:

1. Grammar and spelling: ChatGPT can serve to verify the grammar and spelling accuracy within articles, detecting common mistakes like misspellings, improper punctuation, and inconsistencies in subject-verb agreement.
2. Style and consistency: ChatGPT assists in maintaining the consistency of articles in terms of their style and tone, highlighting any deviations and proposing adjustments to ensure a cohesive read.
3. Fact-checking: ChatGPT aids in fact-checking articles by pinpointing any factual inaccuracies or discrepancies, and it can also suggest additional sources for comprehensive research, thus upholding the accuracy of articles.
4. Clarity and readability: ChatGPT contributes to enhancing the clarity and readability of articles by identifying areas of linguistic complexity and recommending simpler alternatives. Additionally, it can flag sections that might pose challenges for the intended audience.
5. Plagiarism detection: ChatGPT offers a means to scan articles for plagiarism, comparing them against other sources and flagging any instances of similarity in language.

It's crucial to acknowledge that while ChatGPT can be a valuable asset in the editing and proofreading process, it should not be solely relied upon for ensuring the quality and precision of articles. Human editors and proofreaders remain indispensable in guaranteeing thorough review and editing in journalism.

4

Fact-checking with ChatGPT

Fact-checking is an essential aspect of journalism, and artificial intelligence (AI) can contribute to this process by assisting journalists in verifying the accuracy of reported information. ChatGPT, for instance, can aid in fact-checking by cross-referencing data with credible sources and detecting inconsistencies or inaccuracies. For instance, a journalist might input a statement from a source, and ChatGPT could scrutinize it, seeking supporting evidence or discrepancies within the given information. While AI-powered fact-checking can enhance efficiency and accuracy for journalists, it's crucial to remember that AI isn't flawless and should always be supplemented with human expertise and critical thinking abilities.

Utilizing AI for Information Validation

ChatGPT's language processing capabilities enable it to validate information and fact-check articles by analyzing text and comparing it with reliable sources. A journalist could input a claim into ChatGPT, tasking it with verifying its accuracy by cross-referencing with reputable sources. Subsequently, ChatGPT could present a list of sources supporting or contradicting the claim, empowering the journalist to assess the information's accuracy and make any necessary adjustments. Furthermore, ChatGPT could assist in flagging potential instances of bias or propaganda in news articles, aiding journalists in upholding objectivity and integrity in their reporting.

Detecting Fake News and Misinformation

ChatGPT possesses the capability to scrutinize text and discern patterns indicative of misinformation or fake news. Here are several methods through which ChatGPT can contribute to identifying misinformation and fake news:

1. Source verification: ChatGPT can evaluate the credibility of a news story's source by comparing it with established reliable sources.
2. Content analysis: ChatGPT can scrutinize the content of news stories to identify potentially false or misleading claims.
3. Fact-checking: ChatGPT can verify the accuracy of statements in news stories by comparing them with established facts and statistics.
4. Cross-referencing: ChatGPT can cross-check information from multiple sources to identify inaccuracies and inconsistencies.
5. Bias detection: ChatGPT can analyze the language and tone of news articles to identify underlying biases or agendas.

It's important to recognize that ChatGPT serves as a tool and should be used alongside human judgment and critical thinking when evaluating the credibility of news stories and articles.

5

Using ChatGPT for Interviews and Reporting

Journalists can leverage ChatGPT effectively in conducting interviews and gathering information for their articles. Here's how ChatGPT can aid in the interviewing and reporting process:

1. Understanding interviewees: ChatGPT can furnish journalists with background details about the individuals they're interviewing, such as their educational background and work experience. This information helps journalists formulate more insightful questions and conduct better-informed interviews.
2. Formulating interview questions: ChatGPT can suggest relevant topics and follow-up questions, ensuring that journalists cover all essential aspects during interviews and don't overlook important details.
3. Facilitating virtual interviews: As remote work becomes more prevalent, ChatGPT can offer guidance on phrasing questions and responding to answers in virtual settings, thereby assisting journalists in conducting interviews effectively online or over the phone.
4. Transcription support: ChatGPT can aid in transcribing interviews, freeing up journalists' time to focus on analyzing the interview content.

5. Language translation: ChatGPT can translate interviews conducted in different languages into English or another language familiar to the journalist, enhancing accessibility and understanding.
6. Reporting aid: ChatGPT can help journalists generate summaries of information and even draft news reports based on the insights gathered from interviews.

Overall, ChatGPT serves as a valuable asset for journalists in the interview and reporting process. However, it's crucial for journalists to use AI tools responsibly and critically evaluate the information provided to ensure accuracy and fairness in their reporting.

Preparing for Interviews with AI

Preparing for interviews with AI can significantly benefit journalists by saving time and improving the likelihood of a successful interview. ChatGPT offers assistance in various aspects, including generating interview questions, researching interviewees' backgrounds, and identifying areas of interest.

To prepare for an interview with ChatGPT, journalists can begin by researching the interviewee's professional background, including past experiences and notable projects. They can then compile a list of potential questions, utilizing ChatGPT to refine and expand the list as necessary.

During the interview, journalists can employ ChatGPT to transcribe the conversation, highlight key points, and analyze the interviewee's tone and body language for potential follow-up inquiries.

Post-interview, ChatGPT can aid in organizing and summarizing gathered information, as well as identifying potential story angles. In summary, AI streamlines the interview process and offers valuable insights for journalists.

Utilizing ChatGPT for Live Reporting and Transcription

ChatGPT offers versatile support for live reporting and transcription tasks. It excels in transcribing live occurrences like press briefings, speeches, and interviews, delivering instant transcripts crucial for journalistic endeavors. Furthermore, ChatGPT aids journalists in managing multiple data sources concurrently, monitoring social media updates, live feeds, and various data outlets to provide real-time updates and notifications.

Beyond live reporting, ChatGPT streamlines the transcription process for pre-recorded interviews and multimedia content. This efficiency translates to considerable time and energy savings for journalists, enabling them to prioritize content analysis and reporting over transcription duties.

Moreover, ChatGPT facilitates the generation of concise summaries for lengthy materials such as reports or research papers. This feature proves invaluable in time-sensitive situations or when tackling intricate subjects requiring extensive research and analysis.

6

Utilizing ChatGPT for Data Journalism and Visualization

Data journalism encompasses the process of gathering, analyzing, and presenting data to unveil narratives or reveal trends and patterns. ChatGPT serves as a valuable aid for journalists in expediting and streamlining these tasks.

Data Analysis with ChatGPT: Journalists harness ChatGPT's capabilities to scrutinize extensive datasets, spanning from governmental to social media data. This enables them to swiftly discern patterns and trends within the data, enhancing the narrative quality of their stories.

Data Visualization with ChatGPT: Furthermore, ChatGPT facilitates the creation of data visualizations, including charts, graphs, and interactive graphics. These visual aids serve to simplify comprehension of intricate datasets, enriching the story's context and depth.

Fact-checking with ChatGPT: Beyond data analysis and visualization, ChatGPT also proves invaluable in fact-checking endeavors, scrutinizing statistics and claims propagated in speeches and public statements. Journalists leverage ChatGPT to promptly verify information, ensuring the accuracy of their reporting.

Story Generation with ChatGPT: Lastly, ChatGPT aids in generating fresh story ideas grounded in data trends and patterns. By leveraging ChatGPT's capabilities, journalists can uncover compelling topics and angles that might have otherwise eluded them.

Overall, ChatGPT emerges as a potent ally for data journalists, empowering them to unearth novel insights, verify facts, and craft more compelling narratives. However, responsible usage and verification of AI outputs remain imperative.

Leveraging AI for Analyzing Extensive Data Sets

In data journalism, ChatGPT plays a pivotal role in analyzing large datasets. Its proficiency in comprehending and processing natural language facilitates the extraction of pertinent information and insights from vast data troves. For instance, ChatGPT aids in scrutinizing political speeches, social media trends, and public records to discern relevant patterns and trends for specific stories.

Moreover, ChatGPT facilitates the creation of data visualizations, such as charts and graphs, enhancing reader comprehension of complex datasets. By employing natural language queries to pinpoint crucial data points and trends, ChatGPT simplifies the process of creating compelling visual aids for effectively communicating findings to the audience.

Furthermore, ChatGPT supports data mining endeavors, enabling journalists to uncover concealed connections or correlations within extensive datasets. Particularly in investigative journalism, where uncovering hidden links between individuals, organizations, or events is crucial, ChatGPT's ability to analyze natural language text and grasp contextual nuances proves invaluable in identifying significant leads and piecing together intricate narratives.

Utilizing ChatGPT for Data Visualization

ChatGPT is capable of aiding in the creation of data visualizations by suggesting suitable types of charts, graphs, or visual representations based on the nature of the data. It can also offer assistance with the labeling and formatting aspects of the visualizations. Moreover, ChatGPT can propose methods for presenting data in a manner that is both informative and captivating for the audience. Nevertheless, it's crucial to understand that ChatGPT is not designed as a data analysis tool, and it shouldn't be the sole basis for making data-driven decisions. Verifying the accuracy of data and ensuring that the visualizations are correctly labeled and interpreted remains essential.

7

Social Media and Citizen Journalism

The advent of social media has completely transformed the landscape of news consumption, giving rise to citizen journalism as a potent force within the field. Citizen journalism involves ordinary individuals participating in the collection, reporting, and sharing of news and information. Platforms like Twitter, Facebook, and YouTube have significantly facilitated this process, enabling citizens to disseminate news globally with unprecedented ease.

ChatGPT can play a pivotal role in monitoring social media trends and engaging with both the public and citizen journalists. Leveraging its capacity to analyze extensive datasets and discern patterns, ChatGPT aids journalists in staying abreast of breaking news and emerging themes. Furthermore, it assists in fact-checking and source verification.

Moreover, ChatGPT serves as a platform for journalists to interact with their audience and citizen reporters, fostering discussion and soliciting feedback in real-time. This interaction cultivates trust and a sense of community around the news being shared.

Additionally, ChatGPT proves instrumental in identifying and tracking social media influencers and opinion leaders. By scrutinizing social media data and recognizing patterns of influence, journalists gain deeper insights into the underlying social dynamics, enabling them to craft stories that resonate with their audience.

Monitoring Social Media Trends with ChatGPT

ChatGPT emerges as a robust tool for monitoring social media trends and conversations. Its natural language processing capabilities empower it to swiftly navigate vast troves of social media data, pinpointing relevant trends and topics.

One effective method involves configuring ChatGPT to conduct custom searches targeting specific keywords or hashtags pertinent to one's industry or brand. Subsequently, ChatGPT analyzes resulting social media posts, offering insights into prevailing discussions surrounding those subjects.

Alternatively, employing ChatGPT for sentiment analysis enables the examination of language and tone within social media posts, discerning whether they convey positivity, negativity, or neutrality. This facilitates gauging online perceptions of one's brand and identifying potential issues requiring attention.

In conclusion, ChatGPT serves as a valuable asset for journalists seeking to remain informed about the latest social media trends and monitor pertinent conversations relevant to their reporting endeavors.

SOCIAL MEDIA AND CITIZEN JOURNALISM

Engaging with the Public and Amateur Reporters

Utilizing ChatGPT can support journalists in interacting with the public and amateur reporters through various means:

1. Idea Generation: ChatGPT can aid journalists in conceiving fresh and original story concepts by examining current trends, public opinion, and related factors.
2. Verification: ChatGPT can swiftly cross-check information sourced from social media or other outlets, enabling journalists to confirm the authenticity of a story prior to publication.
3. Source Identification: ChatGPT can assist journalists in pinpointing potential sources for a story, considering their expertise, location, or other relevant criteria.
4. Social Media Surveillance: ChatGPT can actively monitor social media platforms for references to specific topics, brands, or events, enabling journalists to keep abreast of unfolding news and public sentiment.
5. Language Translation: ChatGPT can facilitate the translation of social media content or other materials across different languages, simplifying journalists' access to international developments and trends.

In essence, ChatGPT offers journalists the means to stay attuned to emerging patterns and breaking news, establish connections with fresh sources, and uphold the accuracy and comprehensiveness of their reporting.

8

Crisis Reporting and Risk Management

Reporting on crises and managing risks are crucial aspects of journalism that demand meticulous planning, rapid adaptability, and sharp decision-making skills. Artificial intelligence (AI) offers valuable support to journalists, enabling them to streamline their reporting procedures and access crucial information more swiftly during critical situations.

AI can aid in crisis reporting by sifting through social media and other online platforms for breaking news and real-time updates. By programming AI systems like ChatGPT to track specific keywords and phrases across various sources, journalists can receive timely alerts about relevant developments, proving especially beneficial during natural disasters, political turmoil, and other emergencies where up-to-date information is vital.

Moreover, AI contributes to risk management by pinpointing potential threats and vulnerabilities that journalists might encounter during their coverage. For instance, ChatGPT can analyze news articles, social media posts, and other data sources to identify hazardous areas, volatile circumstances, and other risks journalists might face. By delivering this information in real-time, AI assists journalists in making well-informed decisions about where and how to report, minimizing the risk of harm or danger.

Additionally, AI assists in crisis reporting by facilitating the management of vast amounts of data and information. In times of crisis, journalists often need to sift through extensive datasets, reports, and other materials to construct a coherent narrative. AI streamlines this process by automating data analysis and organization, enabling journalists to swiftly identify trends, patterns, and other crucial information.

While AI serves as a valuable tool in crisis reporting and risk management, it is imperative for journalists to utilize these technologies responsibly and ethically. Journalists must uphold principles of source verification, fact-checking, and accuracy in their reporting. Furthermore, transparency regarding the use of AI is essential to foster trust with audiences and uphold the integrity of journalistic work.

Utilizing ChatGPT for Swift Reporting

ChatGPT offers a valuable resource for swift reporting amid emergencies. Journalists can harness AI to swiftly monitor social media and other platforms, swiftly identifying potential breaking news stories. Leveraging ChatGPT, they can analyze data, detect patterns, and uncover trends and leads efficiently. AI-powered chatbots can also aid journalists in addressing common inquiries and disseminating crucial information to the public during crises. Furthermore, AI plays a role in risk management by furnishing journalists with insights into potential safety hazards and furnishing recommendations for ensuring safety during reporting endeavors. Overall, ChatGPT serves as a potent instrument for journalists requiring prompt and precise responses to unfolding news events or emergencies.

Evaluating Hazards and Ensuring Safety in Conflict Zones

As an AI language model, I lack the capacity to evaluate risks or provide safety counsel in conflict zones, as this necessitates specialized expertise and knowledge. It's imperative to seek guidance from seasoned journalists and experts in conflict reporting, individuals well-versed in navigating these environments. They offer insights into best practices, conduct risk assessments, and advise on safety protocols, ensuring the welfare of reporters and upholding the accuracy and integrity of reported information. Moreover, there exist organizations specializing in training journalists for high-risk regions, providing invaluable guidance and resources on this crucial subject matter.

9

Ethical Concerns in AI-Aided Journalism

Similar to any application of artificial intelligence, ethical considerations emerge when employing ChatGPT for journalism. Here are several crucial aspects to take into account:

1. Unbiased Representation: The effectiveness of AI models hinges on the quality of their training data. If this data carries biases, the AI output may also reflect them. Thus, it's vital to ensure that the training data encompasses diverse perspectives and experiences.
2. Privacy Preservation: When utilizing AI for data analysis or information gathering, privacy concerns come to the forefront. Adherence to relevant data protection laws and transparency with the audience regarding data usage are imperative.
3. Precision: Although AI serves as a robust tool for information analysis and summarization, it isn't flawless. Hence, meticulous fact-checking and verification are essential before publishing any content, particularly when AI aids in data collection or analysis.
4. Openness: When employing AI for content generation or reporting assistance, disclosing this aspect to the audience is crucial. This fosters trust and ensures the authenticity and reliability of reporting.
5. Accountability: Ultimately, journalists bear responsibility for their

published content, irrespective of AI involvement. Thus, it's essential to contemplate the impact of reporting and ensure fairness, accuracy, and respectfulness toward all concerned parties.

By adhering to these considerations and utilizing AI tools conscientiously, journalists can leverage technology's potential to enrich their reporting and engage new audiences.

Ensuring Ethical Implementation of AI in Journalism

Just like any other technological advancement, the integration of AI into journalism necessitates ethical deliberation to safeguard the integrity of journalistic practices. The following are some fundamental ethical considerations for incorporating AI into journalism:

1. Precision: Content generated by AI should uphold accuracy, impartiality, and factual correctness. Journalists must not solely rely on AI-generated content without verifying its authenticity and precision.
2. Transparency: Journalists should openly acknowledge the use of AI in content generation, such as by adding a disclaimer or tag indicating AI involvement. Transparency fosters trust between journalists and their audience.
3. Inclusivity: AI-generated content should embrace diversity and encompass varied perspectives. Journalists ought to refrain from utilizing AI in manners that perpetuate stereotypes or biases.
4. Responsibility: Journalists are accountable for the AI-generated content they produce, ensuring alignment with journalistic standards and ethics.
5. Human Judgment: Despite AI aiding in information gathering and processing, human judgment remains paramount in deciding which

stories to cover and how to present them.
6. Privacy: Journalists must be cautious of privacy implications when utilizing AI for data analysis, ensuring compliance with data protection regulations and ethical data usage.

In essence, responsible utilization of AI in journalism necessitates striking a balance between the efficiency and precision offered by AI and the ethical considerations that must be upheld.

Addressing Bias, Privacy, and Ethics in AI Applications

It's imperative to tackle bias, privacy, and ethical concerns in AI applications to uphold responsible usage and safeguard public interests. AI tools like ChatGPT learn from extensive datasets to make decisions, yet they may inadvertently perpetuate biases present in the data, leading to discrimination. Therefore, it's crucial to detect and rectify biases, particularly in applications affecting vulnerable societal groups, such as journalism.

Privacy poses another significant challenge in AI-assisted journalism. Tools like ChatGPT rely on large datasets containing sensitive personal information, necessitating journalists to ensure secure data collection, storage, and anonymization to protect individuals' privacy.

Ethical considerations are paramount when employing AI tools in journalism. Journalists must refrain from using AI to propagate fake news or manipulate public opinion. Transparent disclosure of AI usage and human editorial oversight are essential to maintain the highest standards of accuracy and integrity.

While AI tools like ChatGPT hold promise in revolutionizing journalism by enhancing speed, efficiency, and accessibility, it's imperative to address potential biases, privacy concerns, and ethical considerations to ensure their responsible and ethical utilization.

10

Looking Ahead: ChatGPT and the Future of Journalism

Peering into the future, the trajectory of journalism intertwines significantly with AI, a realm where certainty remains elusive for ChatGPT. Nevertheless, the impact of AI on journalism is undeniable. Potential forthcoming developments include:

1. Advancements in AI tools tailored for research and investigation, empowering journalists to unearth fresh narratives and glean profound insights from data.
2. Heightened integration of AI for fact-checking and authentication, serving as a bulwark against the proliferation of fabricated news and misinformation.
3. Expanded utilization of AI for automated content generation, spanning news articles and synopses, liberating journalists to delve into more comprehensive reporting.
4. Persistent ascent of citizen journalism and social media platforms, ushering in novel hurdles and prospects for journalists to interact with their audience and report on unfolding events in real-time.
5. Ongoing deliberations and deliberations concerning the ethical ramifi-

cations of AI deployment in journalism, encompassing concerns such as bias, privacy infringements, and fostering accountability.

In essence, AI is poised to assume an increasingly pivotal role in journalism, facilitating enhanced efficiency for journalists, facilitating access to novel information sources, and enriching audience engagement with more precise and captivating content. Nevertheless, akin to any nascent technology, journalists must approach AI with a discerning gaze, cognizant of the potential perils and obstacles entailed in its application.

Emerging Trends and Predictions for the Future

The landscape of AI in journalism is marked by various current trends and future projections:

1. Data-centric journalism: As data becomes more accessible and AI tools for analysis advance, data-driven journalism gains traction. AI aids in uncovering hidden patterns and trends within vast datasets, enhancing the accuracy of reporting.
2. Automated news production: AI is already employed to generate news articles, a trend expected to persist. While AI-written content may lack human creativity, it offers rapid and efficient news production.
3. Fact-validation: AI-driven fact-checking tools are evolving, enabling swift and precise verification of information by news outlets.
4. Personalization: AI facilitates content customization for individual users, enhancing engagement and loyalty, albeit raising concerns regarding potential echo chamber effects.
5. Chatbots: News organizations utilize AI-powered chatbots to interact with readers and deliver personalized news and information.

6. Virtual and augmented reality: News outlets employ VR and AR technologies to offer immersive experiences to readers, a trend anticipated to grow alongside technological advancements.
7. Ethics and transparency: With AI's increasing integration in journalism, the necessity for transparency and ethical guidelines becomes imperative to ensure unbiased and responsible usage.

Overall, AI is poised to assume a greater role in journalism in the forthcoming years. Despite concerns surrounding bias and inaccuracies, the benefits of AI in terms of speed, accuracy, and efficiency remain undeniable.

Preparation for an AI-Driven Journalism Landscape

As artificial intelligence (AI) continues to evolve and pervade various facets of society, its significance in journalism amplifies. Capable of processing large datasets, automating tasks, and providing insights, AI is revolutionizing journalistic practices.

A prominent trend in AI-driven journalism involves the utilization of chatbots and natural language processing (NLP) to enhance reader engagement and personalization. Chatbots deliver news, offer recommendations, and engage in conversations with users, while NLP extracts insights and generates content from extensive text data.

Another trend is data-driven journalism, leveraging AI to analyze and visualize data, uncovering trends and presenting information in accessible formats.

AI also automates tasks like transcription and fact-checking, enabling journalists to focus on critical aspects of their work. Additionally, it aids in monitoring social media for breaking news and user-generated content, ensuring journalists stay informed.

As AI progresses, its role in journalism will likely expand. However, ethical considerations regarding bias, privacy, and transparency must be prioritized. AI should augment journalistic efforts, not replace them.

Here's a tailored prompt for journalists:

Compose a piece using this precise prompt in GPT Chat. Then experiment with altering the terms enclosed in " " to suit your preferences. This prompt is especially beneficial for journalists, serving as a potent tool. Prompt: Assume the role of a journalist and craft an article titled "Leading Urban Centers in the United States," targeting a demographic of "males aged 50 and above." Your objective is to "enhance the reputations of these cities." The article should follow this outline: Title, introduction, 1 H2 section, 1 H3 section. The H3 sections will serve as subsections of the H2 sections. Format the article using markdown, employing a "polished" writing style, an "appealing" tone, and a "relaxed" conversational approach.

www.ingramcontent.com/pod-product-compliance
Lightning Source LLC
LaVergne TN
LVHW021050100526
838202LV00082B/5415